JIM THORPE
The World's Greatest Athlete

by Eric Oatman

Scott Foresman
is an imprint of

PEARSON

Glenview, Illinois • Boston, Massachusetts • Chandler, Arizona
Upper Saddle River, New Jersey

Photo locators denoted as follows: Top (T), Center (C), Bottom (B), Left (L), Right (R), Background (Bkgd)

Opener: Corbis; 1 Corbis; 5 Getty Images; 8 Denver Public Library; 10 Getty Images; 11 Corbis; 13 Corbis; 15 Getty Images; 17 Corbis; 18 Corbis; 21 Getty Images

ISBN 13: 978-0-328-51948-4
ISBN 10:   0-328-51948-0

3 4 5 6 7 8 9 10 V0N4 13 12 11 10

~ Jim Thorpe ~

One day, in 1907, in Carlisle, Pennsylvania, a young man walked past several high jumpers and their coach. The jumpers were having trouble getting over the bar.

The young man asked the coach if he could try. The coach was surprised that he wanted to try in work clothes—overalls and heavy work boots—but the coach said he could. He warned the young man that the bar was almost six feet off the ground. The young man stepped back, ran at the bar, and cleared it easily.

The coach, a man named Pop Warner, could not believe it! He immediately wanted the young man on his track team.

The young man's name was Jim Thorpe. Soon he was wearing the uniform of the Carlisle Indian Industrial School, and winning almost every event he entered.

Jim Thorpe loved to compete.

~ Chasing Horses ~

Jim was born on May 28, 1887, near Prague, Oklahoma. At the time, Oklahoma wasn't a state but was called Indian Territory. The Thorpes, who were Native Americans, lived there on land reserved for members of their group, the Sauk and Fox.

Jim's ancestors were not all Native Americans. His father was part Irish, and his mother was part French. Jim's mother and father were brought up as Native Americans, and so were Jim and his ten brothers and sisters. No one could have been more proud of his Native American roots than Jim.

In work that involved the whole family, Jim's father trained and sold horses. When a horse broke away, Jim would chase and catch it. Those long sprints helped make him stronger and build stamina, the ability to keep going without becoming tired.

He was always willing to take on a physical challenge. He would race his twin brother Charlie from tree to tree, or he would dare his friends to try to throw a stone or hit a baseball farther than he could. When he hunted and fished, he wanted to be the one to bring home the biggest deer and the largest fish. Sometimes he ran the twenty miles from his home to the school and back again at the end of the day.

Jim led Carlisle's football team to victory after victory, making him the nation's most famous football player.

~ The Sauk and Fox Nation ~

Jim Thorpe's roots were in the Sauk and Fox. Until the early 1700s, the Sauk and the Fox were neighbors in the forests of southern Michigan. Driven west by other Native American nations and white settlers, they moved to separate villages on the Illinois side of the Mississippi River. During the early 1800s, they were forced west into Iowa and then into Kansas. They were joined by the government as the Sauk and Fox Nation after 1869, when they were moved to a **reservation** in Indian Territory, which is now Oklahoma. Today fewer than four thousand Sauk and Fox live on or near reservations in Iowa, Kansas, Missouri, and Oklahoma.

In 1880 sixty different nations lived in the Indian Territory. By law, only Native Americans could live there, but during the 1870s and 1880s, white settlers came. At first, U.S. soldiers drove them away, but then the U.S. government changed its mind and let settlers claim western parts of the territory.

Soon after Jim was born, the government divided the land reserved for Native Americans. It gave a 160-acre lot to each family and sold any leftover land. The goal was to turn all Native Americans into farmers. This was because, at the time, most Americans were farmers, and the government wanted Native Americans to adopt the ways of American **society.**

But most Native Americans didn't want to be "Americanized." They preferred to live in traditional ways, on land that belonged to the entire nation. They wanted to maintain their own customs, languages, and beliefs, but, unfortunately, they had little choice. By chopping up the land into lots, the U.S. government did away with some of the Native American customs.

In 1889 the states of Texas, Kansas, Missouri, and Arkansas outlined Indian Territory. At this time the Sauk and Fox Nation owned 750,000 acres of land. Today the Sauk and Fox have only eight hundred acres left. Indian Territory became part of the state of Oklahoma in 1907.

~Indian Territory in 1889 ~

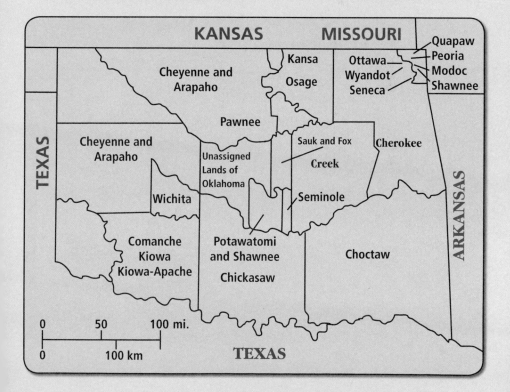

7

As part of the plan to bring Native Americans into the mainstream of American life, the government set up **boarding schools.** Their goal was to teach Native American children to speak English, learn a trade, practice farming, and leave their nation's ways behind them. Jim was only six years old when he was sent to live at a boarding school on the Sauk and Fox reservation. When he was nine, his twin brother, Charlie, died of pneumonia. Jim never got over his brother's death.

Before and after: Like many Carlisle students, Thomas Torlino, of the Diné, arrived at the school in Native American dress. The attempt to "Americanize" him began with a change of clothing and a haircut.

Jim ran away from the school many times. When he was twelve, to keep him in school, his parents sent him to another boarding school farther from home. His mother died while he was there, and he ran away again to work on a horse ranch for a few years.

In 1904, when Jim was seventeen, his father persuaded him to finish his education at the Carlisle Indian Industrial School in Pennsylvania, the nation's oldest boarding school for Native Americans. It educated about one thousand children, who came from more than seventy Native American nations, from grade school through high school.

At school, students were not allowed to speak their native languages. They were taught academic subjects in the morning, and in the afternoons, the boys were taught industrial arts—carpentry, blacksmithing, and the types of **manual** labor used in farming. Girls learned domestic arts, such as sewing and baking.

Shortly after Jim entered Carlisle, his father died. Jim returned to Indian Territory and found work on a farm, but Carlisle lured him back in 1907 when he was twenty years old. That was the year that Pop Warner—and Jim—learned that the young man from Oklahoma had a special gift for sports.

~ The Man Who Invented Modern Football ~

Jim Thorpe's first coach was Glenn "Pop" Warner. Warner coached for many years at many colleges. His teams won three times more games than the number they lost.

Warner was twenty-two years old before he played his first game of football. His teammates at Cornell University called him "Pop" because he was older than any of them. After graduating in 1894, Warner became a coach and worked to improve the sport of football. He taught kickers how to make the ball spiral and sail through the air. He had his players line up with one hand on the ground instead of two. He created shoulder pads and thigh pads to protect the players, and had numbers sewn onto their jerseys. These things had never been done by anyone before.

Jim wanted to play football, even though he seemed to be best at track and field events. He ran, jumped hurdles, high jumped, long jumped, and threw the discus, shot put, and javelin. Pop Warner, however, didn't think that Jim, at 144 pounds, was heavy enough to play college football. Although Carlisle wasn't a college, many of its athletes, like Jim, were old enough to be in college, so most of the school's opponents were college teams. In 1908, Warner finally gave in, and Jim played as a substitute on the football team.

Jim left Carlisle in 1909 to play two seasons of **semiprofessional** baseball in North Carolina. That was not usual for college players; the money was good, and like today, college athletes weren't allowed to play for money.

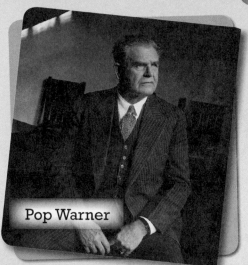

Pop Warner

In 1911 Pop Warner called Jim back to Carlisle. Jim had put on forty pounds of muscle—just what he needed, Pop felt, to excel at football.

In 1894 Pop Warner was captain of the Cornell University football team. After becoming a coach, he put numbers on his players' jerseys so that he could tell them apart.

Jim excelled at football, indeed. As a halfback, he carried the ball from goal line to goal line. No one was better at punting or kicking the ball over a goalpost. On defense, he was one of the team's top tacklers.

In front of a crowd of thirty thousand people at Harvard College, Jim won fame as a football player. That afternoon Jim made a six-point touchdown and four three-point field goals. When the game was over, Harvard had put fifteen points on the scoreboard, and Jim had scored all of Carlisle's eighteen points to win the game. After the season's end, he was named an All-American, one of the best players in the entire country.

Jim also continued to excel at track and field events. Harold Bruce was the track coach at Lafayette College in Easton, Pennsylvania. His team was one of the best in the country. In May 1912, he invited the Carlisle track team to compete at a meet in Easton. The day of the meet, Bruce and forty members of his track team went to the train station to welcome the Carlisle team, and there they saw Warner get off the train with seven young men.

When Bruce asked where Warner's athletes were, Warner said they were standing right next to him.

Bruce could not believe what he was hearing. This was an important day at Lafayette, and the school's graduates were visiting from all over the country. His team had expected a hard-fought meet, but Warner's team of five didn't seem like much of a challenge.

Bruce told Warner that he had forty-six men on his team and that there were eleven events. He said that Warner's five team members would not stand a chance. Not only that, he said the spectators would be bored silly!

Warner had confidence—Bruce's comments did not scare him.

Jim won five events that day and came in third in one other. Two of his teammates finished first and second in three races, and another teammate won the high hurdles. The final score: Carlisle 71, Lafayette 41.

Jim competes in the track and field broad jump event.

A month after the Lafayette track and field meet, Jim sailed to Europe to compete in the 1912 Olympic Games being held in Stockholm, Sweden. Although legend has it that Jim didn't train while on the ship, he ran laps and exercised each day with the rest of the U.S. team.

Once he got to Stockholm, Jim was almost a one-man track team. He competed in two track competitions, the **pentathlon**, which had five events, and the **decathlon**, which had ten events.

The pentathlon required him to compete in the long jump, the javelin throw, the 200-meter dash, the discus throw, and the 1,500-meter run. In the decathlon, Jim faced the long jump, discus, and javelin events again. The seven other events included in this competition were the shot put, the high jump, and the pole vault; the 100-meter, 400-meter, and 1,500-meter foot races; and the 110-meter hurdles.

Jim swept both contests. He earned 8,412 points out of a possible top score of ten thousand in the decathlon, making this performance a record that would not be broken for fifteen years.

After Jim won the decathlon, Sweden's King Gustav V, in praising Jim as the greatest athlete in the world, gave him a drinking cup lined with gold and jewels in the shape of a Viking ship.

Modern-day pentathlete

The pentathlon that Jim Thorpe ran was unlike
the modern version. The modern pentathlon tests
competitors' skills in horseback riding, pistol shooting,
fencing, swimming, and cross-country running.

~ Homecoming ~

Returning to the United States, Jim found even more fame. About fifteen thousand people had turned out in Carlisle, Pennsylvania, to welcome him home. A week later, he was honored at a parade in New York City and then another parade in Philadelphia. Jim had left the United States as the most famous football player in the nation and had returned as its most famous all-around athlete.

That fall Jim was once more the power behind Carlisle's victories on the football field. His team played the U.S. Military Academy (Army) on Thanksgiving Day. In one play, he ran the length of the field—one hundred yards—to score a touchdown. Referees called the play back because a Carlisle player had made an illegal move. On the very next play, Jim ran ninety-seven yards for a touchdown, and this time it counted. The final score was Carlisle 27, Army 6. Jim had scored 22 of those points. Once again, Jim was named to the nation's All-American team.

Sadly, Jim's world came crashing down around him in January 1913. A newspaper reported that he had been paid to play semiprofessional baseball in 1909 and 1910. Olympic rules banned professional athletes from competing against **amateurs.** Jim had known nothing about these rules, but the International Olympic Committee (IOC) demanded that he return his gold medals.

Jim sent his medals and cup to IOC headquarters in Switzerland, where they gathered dust. The public didn't seem to care. They loved Jim and wanted to see him play. Pro teams fought to hire him. He played major league baseball for six years. He played in the outfield for the New York Giants, the Cincinnati Reds, and the Boston Braves.

~ Football and Farewell ~

Jim liked football better than baseball. He played for professional football's best team, the Canton (Ohio) Bulldogs, where Jim then stayed as a player and coach until 1920.

He played football for eight more years. He wore the uniforms of the New York Giants, the Chicago Cardinals, and the Cleveland Tigers. When he retired, he was forty-one years old.

Life after football was difficult for Jim. For someone who had known only sports, it wasn't easy to find work. The Great Depression also made it hard because during this time, many people could not find jobs.

In 1932, the Depression's worst year, U.S. Vice-President Charles Curtis invited Jim to attend the Olympics in Los Angeles. When he arrived, the 105,000 people in the stadium rose to applaud him.

Jim moved many times during the 1930s and 1940s. He worked as an actor in California and on the recreation staff of the Chicago Park District. He helped write a book on the history of the Olympics, became active in the affairs of the Sauk and Fox Nation, and lectured on Native Americans and sports.

Jim Thorpe is ready to tackle.

In 1932 U.S. Vice-President Charles Curtis invited Jim to watch the opening ceremonies of that year's summer Olympics in Los Angeles. Like Jim, Curtis was part Native American.

In 1950 nearly four hundred sportswriters and broadcasters named Jim the most outstanding athlete of the first half of the twentieth century. A movie about his life, *Jim Thorpe All American,* was released in 1951.

Jim died on March 28, 1953, in California. In 1954 two Pennsylvania towns agreed to merge and call the new town Jim Thorpe. Jim is buried there, in the only town in the United States believed to have been named after an athlete.

After his death, recognition of Jim's greatness kept coming. In 1963 he was elected to the National Football League Hall of Fame. In 1982 the IOC realized that it had broken its own rules in taking Jim's medals away and gave copies of them to his family in 1983. Today the college football award for the Best Defensive Back is named after Jim Thorpe.

Honors such as these make it clear that the man who stunned Pop Warner in 1907 with his high jumping skill was one of a kind. He was the greatest athlete that America has ever produced.

Jim hurls a heavy metal ball in the shot put event at the 1912 Olympic Games in Stockholm, Sweden.

Now Try This

Sports World

Jim Thorpe was a top performer in just about every sport he tried. As you know, he was a track and field star. He was also excellent at baseball, basketball, ice hockey, and tennis. He made golfing and figure skating look easy.

How much do you know about these sports and others? Here's your chance to find out!

Research the history of a sport you want to learn about. Jot down your answers to as many of these questions as you can:

- Who invented the sport?
- What equipment is needed to play it?
- Is the sport played in other countries? Where is it played? Do Americans play the sport? If so, when did they begin playing it, and where?
- Why do people like to play the sport or watch it?
- What fun facts might call people's attention to the sport?

Turn what you learn into an advertisement. Make a poster to persuade people to play or watch your sport. Attach a picture of someone playing it. Cut it out from a magazine, download it, or draw one. Use the poster on the next page as a model. After you have finished, display your poster so your classmates can learn about the sport and what makes it fun.

Cricket Rocks!

Worldwide, more people watch cricket than any other sport except soccer!

The annual United States versus Canada cricket match is the oldest international sporting event in the modern world!

English shepherds invented it.
British princes improved it.
More than ten thousand Americans play it today.

Girls play it! Boys play it!
It's fun! You'll love it!

Glossary

amateurs *n.* athletes who play without being paid.

boarding schools *n.* schools with buildings where students live during the school term.

decathlon *n.* a ten-event track and field contest.

manual *adj.* done with the hands.

pentathlon *n.* a five-event track and field contest.

semiprofessional *adj.* getting paid to play a sport part-time.

reservation *n.* land set aside by the government for a special purpose.

society *n.* the people of any particular time or place.